TRYING TO BE HUMAN
ZEN TALKS FROM CHERI HUBER

D0390156

TRYING to be HUMAN

ZEN TALKS
FROM
CHERI HUBER

Edited by Sara Jenkins

Present Perfect Books
Lake Junaluska, North Carolina

Library of Congress Catalog Card Number: 95-68525

Publisher's Cataloging in Publication
(Prepared by Quality Books, Inc.)
Trying to be human: Zen talks from Cheri Huber / edited by Sara Jenkins.
p. cm.
ISBN 0-9630784-1-0
1. Zen Buddhism.   I. Jenkins, Sara.   II. Huber, Cheri.
BQ9266.T79 1995   294.3'927
                        QBI 95-20220

Present Perfect Books

Box 1212, Lake Junaluska, North Carolina 28745

CONTENTS

WILLINGNESS

ALREADY ENLIGHTENED

PREFACE

What could it mean, to "try" to be human?

In this book Cheri Huber mentions the idea that "we are not human beings trying to be spiritual, but spiritual beings trying to be human." That is, instead of striving toward an ideal image of ourselves, we might aim simply to see more clearly what being human is all about, including what impels our striving. In Zen practice we learn that if we pay close attention, sooner or later we discover that there are no differences between "spiritual" and "human." We already are everything we yearn for.

This book is about turning our "trying" in a different direction, then dropping effort altogether as we come to understand that our true nature is goodness. What I have learned about this process is through the Zen Buddhist meditation practice taught by Cheri Huber. The pages that follow present distillations of her teachings.

I met Cheri Huber nine years ago at Southern Dharma Retreat Center. She was there for a month to lead a series of Zen retreats, and I was there working on the staff. At that time, I had firm ideas about how spiritual teachers are different from us regular human beings. As fate would have it (or karma, or plain old circumstance), Cheri and I worked side by side to prepare for her retreat. We scrubbed bathrooms, vacuumed, arranged cushions in the meditation hall, washed dishes, talked and laughed. Thus, I first got to know Cheri not in the role of spiritual teacher but as a regular person. And that experience began to unsettle my notion of spiritual as something other than human.

At the end of the month, Cheri astonished me by saying something like this: "At our Zen Center, someone records the discussions, and the tapes are transcribed, and I am given a stack of paper that purportedly represents what I have said. The stack is growing, and I don't know what to do with it. Every night I look at all that paper and feel vaguely guilty. Now, you're an editor: I am giving that material to you. Do whatever you want with it; publish it with your name on it, or throw it away. I just want it off my bedside table." In my experience, regular human beings tend to cling tooth and nail to "their" words. Being given material for a book along with complete editorial freedom seemed too good to be true. And yet it happened: that first stack of transcripts eventually became *Turning Toward Happiness: Conversations With a Zen Teacher and Her Students.*

That same pattern has been repeated over the years: Cheri acts in ways I consider imprudent, careless, even reckless, but in those very actions offers me what I truly want. The only thing she refuses is to act as an authority for me; she always turns me back to myself.

This book reflects what I have heard and found meaningful and chosen from a variety of Cheri's talks; other people will have heard and understood differently, according to their own practice.

Cheri insists that year in and year out, she says the same things, using different words in different combinations, in her attempts to convey the simple experience of being present that is the totality of Zen practice. What changes is our perception, our understanding, our readiness to know the deeper meaning of what is offered on this path.

The words are like maps showing the location of a buried treasure. At the beginning, the map can appear as a jumble of cryptic hieroglyphs. (I, for one, despaired of ever figuring out how to read it.) But with each step forward, we gain a clearer perspective on where we are, where we have come from, and the meaning of the directions we have been given.

Sometimes the map carries signs of the awesome effort required of those who preceded us on this path — traces of their struggles against doubt and fear and confusion, reflections of their faith and courage and persistence — all of which serve as clues to help us find our way. The map is thus invested with regular human qualities, and eventually we come to know that that is precisely what makes it so precious.

Sometimes the map is revealed as a huge, hilarious joke we catch on to only as we look back and realize there is nowhere to go. The true nature of the map is to help us know this for ourselves, for the ultimate treasure is none other than full awareness of where and who and what we are.

This book is part of the map I have been given, and I pass it on with deep gratitude. ◆

Sara Jenkins

11

ENCOUNTERING THE PATH

Choosing a
Spiritual Path

How does one choose a spiritual path? My recommendation is to go with what appeals to you. By that, I mean something you feel drawn to in your heart — not just because your friends belong or you've heard about this neat monastery in the mountains or people say that teacher is really great. But when something touches you deeply, turn toward that and stick with it.

When it comes to choosing a spiritual path, see if you notice yourself thinking, "Well, you just can't be too cautious about these things." We say no to a lot of things that are perfectly harmless, and might even be helpful, but would not support our egocentric identity. And we say yes to an awful lot of things that are pretty shady, and maybe downright dangerous, but do support our identity. Many of us, for example, make all sorts of life decisions that are not in our own best interest; we will enter into a relationship with no thought at all — or even with full awareness that it is not going to be very good for us. But when it comes to spiritual practice, we are oh-so-very careful.

One way we exercise this kind of caution is by trying to do

spiritual practice through reading books. A particular path sounds interesting, so we spend a week reading about it. But that approach doesn't seem to do anything for us. Now, that's probably the best time to stay with it, but we move on and spend another week on something else. The image that comes to my mind is looking for water by digging a little bit here, then giving up and moving to another spot and digging a little bit there, and never getting deep enough to be anywhere close to water. But if you stop *anywhere* and just keep on digging — staying with it through your impatience and frustration and tiredness and disappointment when your expectations aren't met — sooner or later you will find what you are looking for. ◆

Ending Suffering

My understanding of what the Buddha taught is that there is a reason that suffering happens, and it is possible to end suffering. For me, the easiest way to understand that is recognizing how my suffering arises from wanting something other than what is.

I would not ask you to take my word for this; you have to find out for yourself. In Buddhism we don't proselytize, for the simple reason that no one will do a spiritual practice like this until they have suffered enough. People who are attracted to it only intellectually will use it as one more thing to dabble in, and then they will go on and dabble in something else. And that's fine. Buddhism addresses the issue of ending suffering only if you have suffered enough. It does not say you should do this practice, or only superior people do this practice, or you are going to hell if you do not do this practice.

Encountering the path that leads to ending suffering is sort of like seeing a bicycle for the first time and being told you could get on this contraption and ride it: it sounds incredible, although to anyone who has ridden a bicycle, it is quite obvious that it can be done. But it is one thing to say, "This thing exists, and you can ride it if you want to," and quite another to say, "There is a bicycle, and you *must* ride it, and you're a bad person if you don't." It is the same with this practice. As far as I know, the Buddha never said you *shouldn't* suffer. He just explained how it happens.

Pain is inevitable, and suffering is what happens to you when you resist pain (or any experience). Suffering is when you think there is something wrong with what happens, when you refuse to accept it, when you are separate from your experience. If you break your leg, it is going to hurt. The suffering comes in with the attitude "This is not my correct life experience. I am living a life in which I do not break my leg. There's been a big mistake here."

A common misconception is that you may break your leg, but if you are very advanced spiritually, you will be able to psych yourself out to not feel the pain. Some people see Buddhism as a way to do that, but for me, Buddhism is encouragement to be fully present to whatever you are experiencing. If somebody else can do that trick with the disappearing pain, good for them, but that doesn't help me. Whether I feel the pain or not, the point is that there is no alternative life in which I did not break my leg. So, nothing is a mistake.

The Buddha taught that suffering arises from the illusion of the self as separate from all that is. If you do not believe you are a somebody to whom things are happening, then nothing will happen to you. If we do not take life personally, we are not caught up in thoughts like "This happened to me because of that" and "If only I were this way, then that would not be happening." This kind of struggle against what is — not the pain of a broken leg — is how we suffer.

My teacher used to say that after awakening, everything is exactly the same but completely different. And everybody who has let go of anything knows that is the case. If you have a difficult relationship with a co-worker, for example, and all of a sudden you let go of that difficulty, that person has not changed, but there is no longer any problem because you experience it differently.

We can never end suffering outside of suffering, because the end of suffering is embracing the suffering as it happens. That's why, once we ask, "What do I do?" it's already too late. Fortunately, we can always have another shot at it, because in the next moment the suffering will arise again. This practice involves sitting still as we bring all our suffering to be embraced in compassion. It doesn't always feel like that, but that's what we're moving toward: sitting still in the heart and mind of compassion and drawing into that everything that is *not* that, everything that causes us to leave that compassion, everything we suffer over. That is the practice of ending suffering. ◆

The Conditioned Sense of Self

From the moment we are born, we are being conditioned to see things a certain way, to have certain beliefs and assumptions, to think that certain things are good, real, beautiful, valuable and other things are not. We are conditioned first by our parents, then by society. The messages we internalize from those sources maintain the whole system of our conditioning, which constitutes egocentricity, or the sense of being a separate self.

The process is so pervasive that we are unaware of it. It continues to surprise us that other people don't see things the way we do. To me, it may be entirely obvious that this dog is lovable and that book is brilliant and this food is disgusting and that shirt is the wrong color, and I am shocked and dismayed to learn that you perceive these matters quite differently.

As I look at the world through the filter of my conditioning, my constant referring to the filter — rather than to actuality — is how I know who I am. Who am I? I am the person who finds this dog lovable and that book brilliant and this food disgusting and that shirt the wrong color.

Conditioned responses stand between us and direct experience of the world. If we want to be fully present to what is actually going on, we cannot remain blind to our conditioning. We must see it for what it is and move into the freedom that lies beyond it. Some courage may be required, because if we step outside the conditioned sense of self and ask, Who am I? there is no answer. That sounds scary. But the good news is that once we go beyond our conditioning, the question of who I am never arises. What fills the gap where my identity used to be is simply experience itself. ♦

The Prison We Think of as Home

We cling to the identity provided by our conditioning as if it were life itself, but in fact it is the source of our suffering.

A funny thing — or fascinating or sad, depending on your perspective — is that most people are already in hell, and they are fighting desperately to stay there. Bhagwan Shree Rajneesh said that as long as we stay trapped in our conditioned responses, in the illusion of separateness, we are like people in a prison who have abandoned our own hearts for so long that we have decorated the prison and think of it as our home, and if someone came with a key to let us out, we would kill that person.

Conditioned responses are replayed almost constantly in our minds: from parental messages like "You should know better than that," which undermine our sense of adequacy; to the punitive thoughts we use to try to make ourselves live up to an idea of how we ought to be; to the subtlest of judgments in which we align ourselves with a certain standard and thereby deprive ourselves of everything that doesn't meet that standard. The subjugation we experience through our conditioning is far more cruel than anything anyone else could inflict upon us. It is our very effort to protect ourselves — the misguided attempt to defend the illusion of our separateness — that is the source of our suffering. This is what "delusion" or "ignorance" refers to in Buddhism. This is the prison we think of as home, the bondage we mistake for safety. ♦

The First Psychologist

Much of what we talk about may sound like psychology, but in fact what we are doing here is Buddhism. Our approach is similar to that of the Zen master Bankei, which I think is the essence of Soto Zen: simply taking everyday life and seeing it as the koan, using whatever helps us move beyond our egocentric attachments. So, we talk about the same kinds of things people talk about with their friends or family or counselor or therapist. Whether you call it psychology or Zen, you are going to be working with much the same material.

The process we use, however, is completely different from psychotherapy. The purpose of psychotherapy is to strengthen the ego, and the purpose of spiritual practice is to dissolve the ego. So, while the spiritual teacher is pulling apart the structures of the illusory self, the therapist is putting Band-Aids on to hold it all together. For this reason, to me it seems counterproductive to pursue psychotherapy and spiritual practice at the same time (although I would not want to make a rule about that).

Buddhism has been called the first psychology and the Buddha the first psychologist. What has come down to us of what the Buddha supposedly said suggests that he endlessly scrutinized his own mind, and eventually he saw how it all worked. Now, any of you who examines your own mind that persistently will come to roughly the same conclusions as the Buddha, because you are scrutinizing the same thing: a human being. No matter what angle you are looking from, if you pay attention long enough, you will wake up and see your conditioning for what it is, see the source of your suffering, and see that it is the same for all of us. You will see what the Buddha saw. Then you, too, can acknowledge your own enlightenment. ◆

Nothing To Do

People say to me, "Zen is supposed to be silent. Why are we talking so much?" Yet those same people require fairly regular feedback and pep talks if they are going to stick it out in this practice.

Everything we do besides sitting meditation — discussions, workshops, and so on — is someone's idea of how to make the practice easier, how to make the teachings more accessible. Each person who pursues a practice contributes some insight, a particular approach, or a memorable way of putting something into words, and so after hundreds of years, we have this complex body of ostensibly helpful material. Probably ninety-nine percent of it could be chucked out, and then we could start all over again. But if nothing else, just getting through it all provides a nice challenge in the patience department.

Being a Western teacher in the West, I don't have any idea what it was like in Japan X number of centuries ago. But judging from the stories that have come down to us, it sounds as if people were a lot more motivated then: you read about students wanting to train so desperately that they cut off their arms, begging the Zen master, "Please let me study with you." Those days are over, as far as I can tell. Now people come to spiritual practice with the attitude "What's in this for me? Because right around the block there's another tradition, and with that one, I can get Eternal Peace. What are you offering?" Those old Zen masters used to say, "Just go in, sit down facing the wall, follow your breath, and I'll get back with you in a few months." But that is just not the American way.

So, is there a reason to talk about all this? Absolutely not. Talking simply gives people something to do while they let go of their need to have something to do. We talk until you find the courage to sit.

Thinking there is something to do is a trap. The trick is, when there is a moment of consciousness, to bring your attention back to the present. Anytime you can come back to the here and now, to that experience of well-being, bliss, joy, whatever — do it. You don't have to earn it. You don't have to fix anything that happened in the past, even what just happened in the past second. You don't have to solve any problems. You don't have to think about anything ever again. Just get right here to the present moment, and when the next thought or feeling arises, let it arise within that experience of being fully present.

Whenever you ask yourself, "What should I do?" you can know you are stuck in your conditioning. What we are looking for is what is there when we stop doing everything else. ◆

Having It All

Americans have had the unique experience of getting everything that is supposed to make them happy and finding out it doesn't. When that happens, you figure maybe there's something else to life than just getting what you want all the time.

That something else is finding the joy within oneself, rather than as a result of life circumstances. Life circumstances are always liable to change. If I depend on externals for my well-being, then I am bound to be a victim. But if my well-being comes from within, it does not matter what is going on anywhere else. Each time something happens in a way that doesn't please me, that is my best opportunity to let go of that process of suffering and come back to being with what is.

Ego's job is getting itself through the world with what looks like the best possible deal. "Do I like this? Do I want that? Will this work for me?" Yes to this, no to that: it seems as if this is the key to getting what we want. But, in fact, this *is* the path of suffering — because getting the best deal works only for so long, as we all know if we look honestly at our lives. ◆

The Perfect Person

I would encourage you to jettison your ideals just as quickly as you can — especially your ideals about how someone else should be or about how you should be.

Before I became a spiritual teacher, I knew everything about how spiritual teachers should be. I could have told you how they should think, how they should feel, how they should act, how they should live their lives. But the longer I teach, the less I know about what a spiritual teacher is. Before I became a parent, I knew everything about how children should be brought up. Of course, this was based on my experience as a child, and my experience as a parent was very humbling. It is good to approach spiritual practice with that same attitude of humility: being open to *discovering what it is about* rather than assuming we know.

We want to find the perfect person, the perfect Mom/Dad who will always love us and accept us and embrace us and do what we want so that we will feel good and secure and happy. And we also want to *be* the perfect person so we never have to pay attention to what is actually happening, never have to examine ourselves.

But those attitudes have nothing to do with spiritual practice. If you are waiting for the perfect spiritual teacher to guide you down the perfect path to a perfect realization and a perfected personality, I may be able to save you some time and trouble, because I can assure you that is not going to happen.

We are conditioned to believe that our two choices are to be perfect or not to be perfect. But is that so? Are the alternatives to follow a conditioned belief about perfection or to resign ourselves to being imperfect? Where does the standard for perfection come from?

I would encourage you not to have any preconceived notions about what or how you will be. That way, the entire range of possibilities will be available to you. ♦

A Project for Saving the World

In considering the problems that exist in this world, we somehow maintain the delusion that hatred is helpful. I hate pollution, so the whole time I'm driving my car, I'm hating the traffic and hating the exhaust fumes and feeling, why doesn't the Environmental Protection Agency do something about this? Of course, *I've* got to drive; I lead a busy life. And I have to fly; I know it's ecologically unsound, but how else would I get across the country? So, here we are, trying to figure out who is doing something wrong, who to hate. That is our usual approach to rectifying problems.

But the desire to deal with a problem does not have to be connected to feeling upset about it. That is an important awareness in spiritual practice.

Let's imagine we are a group of people who decide they are going to "save the world" — not because we should, not even because we believe there is anything wrong with the world, but simply because we want to. We might decide that what we want to accomplish is helping orphans in Ethiopia: we will feed and clothe them and provide them with medical care and education.

Now, in taking this on as our project, there are a couple of rules we will adopt: one, we cannot blame anybody else, and two, we cannot involve anybody else. In other words, we have to take complete responsibility. Our first act, then, is not to notify government authorities of their negligence and suggest how much money they should give us to solve this problem.

The motivation for us lies within our own spiritual practice. We suspect that doing this kind of thing in life is a lot more rewarding than going to a job that we don't like just because it pays us a lot of money.

As we pursue this project, we get very excited and enthusiastic about it. That attracts other people; they can see that what we are doing is more fun than what they are doing. Then they want to get involved in our project, so we teach them the two rules and let them play, too.

Remember that we are engaged in this project only because we want to be, not because we are angry and not because we think there is something wrong that we can correct. If we are angry about something, we can work around the clock, sending telegrams, making phone calls, organizing rallies, all that kind of thing. But if we are not upset, the momentum has to come from another source. It has to come from willingness. Rather than simply being carried along by emotion, letting righteous indignation fuel our actions, we must be willing to bring our attention back to the present each and every moment. When we are no longer in that out-of-control state where activity just happens, we have to draw upon a deeper place within ourselves.

We encounter the practical application of this all the time in finding our willingness to meditate. When you first get home after a retreat, that rush of spiritual enthusiasm is so great that you can hardly go to work because you want to meditate all day long. Then that passes, more quickly for some people than for others. After a week, a month, two months, three months, there is no longer a spontaneous sense of "Yes, I want to do this." At that point, you have to find your willingness to do it simply because it is the deepest desire of your heart.

It does not seem to me that we are here to fix the world. It is only an assumption that another world is possible; we have no experience of it ever being any different from the way it is. To my mind, that is the best argument for concentrating on the change we know *is* possible, which is the change that happens to people when they take on something like this project — for their own spiritual practice, as a way of personal transformation. ◆

From God to Garbage and Back

Much of our conditioning is exactly the opposite of what is so. For example, have you noticed how a common response to noticing your own greed is to turn around and be stingy with yourself? A person who has to have lots is a person who feels that they do not have enough, and yet we will respond to that sense of deprivation in ourselves by denying our need and depriving ourselves further, as punishment. We do not expect starving people to share their food; we understand that when they have had plenty to eat and feel sure there will be plenty to eat in the future, then they can be generous. Yet when it comes to ourselves, we can withhold what we need and still expect ourselves to act generously. Then, when we don't act generously, we punish ourselves by thinking we are bad people.

Thinking we are bad is the first error, which we compound by trying to punish our bad self into being good. But that will never, ever work. If we look honestly at ourselves, we will see that it has never worked yet. And it never will. Stinginess cannot beget generosity; cruelty cannot beget kindness. A verse in the Dhammapada says the same thing that Peace Pilgrim said, which in essence is what St. Francis said: Conquer anger through gentleness, unkindness through kindness, greed through generosity, falsehood through truth.

When we are feeling bad about ourselves, we can seem very humble and generous. "Oh, I am just a worthless sinner, I have nothing to offer, I have no good qualities. So, any outhouses you need cleaned?" But we don't want to stick with that position for long. "I'm a piece of garbage," we'll say, and yet somehow manage to turn that into "And I'm very special and I deserve the best of everything and the whole world is being cruel if they don't give it to me."

It comes down to what is going to work for my ego in this moment. Being the best does not always suit the purposes of ego; sometimes being the worst works better in maintaining the illusion of separateness. Right now I don't want to take responsibility, so I'm a piece of garbage. But in the next moment, I deserve the best of everything, so somehow I'm a wonderful person who is misunderstood. I need equal doses of "I'm nothing/I'm everything, I'm the devil/I'm God, I'm awful/I'm perfect." If we look at the two columns at the end of the day, they balance out. Or, if you are on a different time cycle, you may have four or five days of being garbage, and then you will have four or five days of being God.

Now, that is a perfect demonstration of how we are conditioned to see the world in terms of opposites, of duality. And once we have seen it, in all its absurdity, it's not so easy to believe it anymore. ♦

Urgency

My job, as I see it, is to guide people out of being stuck in their conditioning, unable to see the way to the wisdom, love, and compassion of their true nature. Since I am familiar with this path, we can travel it together. I can be helpful because people come to me and ask for that, and anyone can do this for anyone.

But before you start thinking of offering your spiritual knowledge to your loved ones, keep in mind that it is best if people ask.

Also, to let you in on one of the secrets of this job: I try not to tell people anything I really want to tell them. If I think I have something this person needs to know — I have identified their problem, I've got the solution, and when I give them this information they will be fixed — if I feel some urgency about it, I refrain from saying anything. I just store that for my own meditation, because I have a good idea who might need to spend some time with this issue, and it's not the other person. ◆

Change

For each of us there is one person whose suffering we can end, and that is ourselves. No matter how much I love you or you love me, I cannot end your suffering, and you cannot end mine. That's just how it is. (In fact, sometimes it seems like the more we love somebody, the more we add to their suffering, but that's a different discussion.)

When we talk about changing other people, that supposes the existence of someone else who is separate from this self. But if, as the Buddha taught, that is not the case, then if I change, it affects the entire universe.

It is good to keep in mind that what you are really learning about is you. Each person with whom you come into contact, each event in your life, simply mirrors you. In the same way, you mirror others. That is what we do with one another: we act as mirrors. To me, that is quite satisfying.

We are drawn to spiritual practice because we want to change ourselves. We have been trying to change ourselves forever, and it has never worked. But it is the "I" who wants to change who is the only problem; that illusion of separateness is the only thing wrong.

In this practice of coming back to the oneness of each moment, again and again, sitting on the cushion with compassion for all our suffering, the illusion loses its grip. And in a way we never imagined, we are changed. ♦

Reading and Sitting

My recommendation is, never read without meditating first. We often find time to read about spiritual practice but cannot find time to sit on that cushion. Think of reading as a supplement to sitting meditation, not a substitute for it. Reading is tempting because when we read, we feel inspired, and when we sit, we feel fidgety. We think, "I'll read this inspiring book, and it will put me right into the mind of meditation. Then I can go outside and focus my attention on the clouds going by. That's almost the same as meditation." But it's not.

Sitting on the cushion, maintaining the posture, following the breath, paying attention: that's what this practice is. Most people, however, will read a lot of books before they are willing to do the simple thing that will end their suffering.

One reason to always meditate before reading is that whatever you read will tend to be received at a deeper level (which might change your reading habits). But mainly it's that you will be giving priority to what will be most helpful in your practice, which is — yes — sitting meditation. ♦

Don't Wait

I would encourage everyone interested in a spiritual practice in this lifetime not to procrastinate.

We tend to think that we need to be close to death before we give up the suffering. But it makes much more sense to end the suffering as quickly as possible and live as much of our lives as possible in happiness. There is simply no intelligent reason to live a life of suffering.

Do not assume that you have forever. If spiritual practice is important to you, make it important. Spiritual practice is like marriage in that many people don't realize how important it is until it is over. It gets postponed again and again; people say, "Spiritual practice is very important to me, and I'm going to get to it just as soon as I . . . ," and there's always something.

So, I like to remind people that we cannot know how much time we have, and it is important to live life where your heart is. ♦

WILLINGNESS

Sitting Meditation

What do I need to learn for my life to work? The answer to that question is not what we want to hear.

In the beginning, this practice seems to have all sorts of fascinating ways of explaining what it is that you need to know to make your life work. But what we don't hear — and we don't hear it because we don't want to, and everybody is in this same boat — is that meditation is what works.

All this other stuff we do fills the time until people get it that this is in fact a meditation practice. I keep hoping that eventually the point will come when we have looked at everything under the sun from every possible perspective, and there will be nothing left for me to say except that meditation is the answer.

If there were another way to do it besides sitting on the cushion, trust me, I would have been doing it by now. I am no more enamored of sitting than anyone else. But sitting on the cushion is the way. You don't have to like it, you don't have to want to do it, you don't have to feel successful while you do it, you don't have to have good meditations. All you have to do is sit there, and the magic works. People who have been sitting for a while always nod their heads when I say this.

Let's say I have defined a certain pattern of behavior as the major reason my life isn't working the way I want it to. How do we work with patterns of behavior in spiritual practice? Exactly the same way as we sit on the cushion. We continue to be willing to come back to this moment and to pay attention. We continue to be willing to be present to whatever happens. We question, we examine. We return to the breath, over and over and over again. ◆

Fear

When you sit still with compulsive behavior, what you confront is the underlying fear. Then you are onto something manageable.

Through meditating you will be able to experience the sensation in your body that you call fear. What would that sensation be without the belief system that goes with it? What is fear, actually?

"Well, I'm afraid I'm going to die." You are going to die, that's true. Are you dying in this moment? Not so that it shows.

So, is the fear an experience you are having, or an idea you are holding? What would that sensation be without that idea, the label, those beliefs, that conditioning? You can begin to learn that in meditation.

Watch how the process works in your mind. You wake up in the morning and everything is fine. Then a thought comes through, the fear follows it, the voices kick in with your conditioned responses, and you are off and running straight into suffering.

In meditation you begin to watch that kind of process. You see the relationship between the sensation and that label; you see your reaction and the belief system that goes with it. And you begin to suspect that what's really going on has nothing to do with what you think is going on. You begin to see that there are certain times when these patterns happen; you notice that they are in fact patterns, and you no longer believe them. You bring your attention back closer and closer to the sensation that actually triggers the pattern. And you discover that there is no such thing as fear. ♦

Disidentification
Versus Dissociation

The process we focus on in this practice is disidentification from the conditioned sense of self. This is in no way similar to dissociating from, say, childhood experiences that were too painful to bear.

The way we disidentify is by bringing the attention back to the breath. That does not prevent anything from happening. It is an experience of being completely open. When you bring your attention to the breath, you have no defenses. There is nothing to keep anything from arising. With dissociation, however, you wall yourself off so that you are protected, so that your reality contains certain things and not other things.

When someone's reason for wanting to meditate is to feel less stressed, I encourage them to look elsewhere. In some types of meditation you focus on one thing that blocks out everything else, but in our type of meditation, if you try not to think about something, that thing will be right there. If you are sitting still and paying attention, when something arises, you are present to it, and you see what there is to see.

At first, we tend to let what we see take us away from the present. And when something really difficult arises, we may believe we should let the whole drama play so we can examine it, follow it out all the way. But we don't have to meditate very long before we follow out an awful lot of the same stories — the ones that run through our heads all the time.

Now, psychotherapists get concerned that people will repress something or "stuff" their emotions. Here is the rule of thumb I offer people who worry about this: follow a story twice. Let the whole drama play through twice. Anything after that is not going to be fruitful.

After you have run through a story two times and you feel comfortable that you know how it goes, the next time it arises, simply stay present and attend to it. The more open you are, the more you will see, and then you can just let it pass away. It will arise again, many times, and you can look at it again. But each time it arises, it is a little different, you are a little different, the moment is a little different, so you experience something different. Just stay with that. Thinking about it is not helpful. When you are totally present to it, the moment something arises is the best you are ever going to get. That is your best chance to see it for what it is, to see through it.

If we sit with that attitude of mind, with the willingness to be present to whatever arises, everything will arise, including all those things we thought we left back in our childhood, insulated in that protected, walled-off space. That is why it is critical to have the practice to come back to, because only when we are disidentified can we allow all those things to be embraced and acknowledged and seen clearly. So, the safest way to address these issues is from that centered place, the mind of meditation.

If we leave that willingness, that openness, that acceptance, and let small mind take over, we will identify with either the child who had the experience, which is terrifying, or with the parental figure who was doing whatever it was that caused the child to escape into that walled-off place of dissociation.

To me, the really wondrous part of this practice is this. We start out seeing whatever is on the surface: in a childhood trauma, say, the surface is everything we know about it from our adult perspective. As we continue to sit and be open, a little piece of our adult version of the story will fall away, and we will see through to something we had not been able to acknowledge before. And then another little piece will fall away, and we will see something else, and as we continue to sit, more falls away, and we see more clearly. If we saw it all the first time we sat down, it would be horrible, because we would not be ready to see it. But as we build faith and confidence that the mind of meditation can embrace whatever comes up in our life experience, then when we get to the deep-down dark and scary stuff, we know that we are ready to see and embrace that and let it out.

Many people quit meditation practice for this very reason: it opens the door to everything we ever tried not to face. And from a Buddhist perspective, we aren't talking about just one childhood; we are talking about lifetime upon lifetime, eons of suffering. All of it will find its way into our awareness if we sit still with it long enough, and allowing that to happen is the only way it will be healed. ◆

Egocentricity

Egocentricity is the process of wanting something other than what is. Egocentricity means there is an "I" who is separate from everything else and doesn't like it; one thing is happening, but I want a different thing to be happening. Egocentricity is that constant concern with how I feel, what I think, what I'm doing, what I want — looking at what is and seeing it as inadequate. My identity is maintained by the struggle of wanting something other than what is; that is how I continue to know myself.

This practice involves finding a willingness to suffer in order to end our suffering. Instead of spending our time trying to avoid suffering, we just find the willingness to go directly into it. Whenever anything causes us to suffer, we can know two things: suffering is the same as egocentricity, and when it arises, that is our best opportunity to end suffering. As we open to our suffering, as we embrace it, as we accept it, our relationship to it changes. It is no longer something horrible, something to escape from. Suffering becomes just another opportunity, another chance for freedom.

Please find out about that for yourself. ◆

Separateness

 Where on earth would we find a boundary between us? Would it be the air between us that we both breathe? Would it be the skin on my body that is participating in the exact same atmosphere as the skin on your body?

The idea of separateness is something we have to make up, so we say everything that connects us doesn't count because we can't see it. Of course, if the air weren't there all of a sudden, it would become important in a hurry. But for right now, we choose not to pay attention to it.

Look and see how you make up separateness within yourself. Look for your sense of "self" and "other." Notice how within yourself, there are many selves. Inside or outside yourself, see if you can find a boundary. ◆

Cutting Through Ego Maintenance Systems

Egocentricity, the illusion of separateness, requires constant maintenance. What maintains it is that endless buzz-buzz-buzz in our minds, telling us who we are, who they are, what we are doing, what is important, where we are going next — creating that subject-object relationship in every split second. The continual brainwashing that maintains our identity is like a tape loop.

But every time we pay attention, every time we are present, it is like cutting through that tape. Of course, the tape is instantly spliced back together again, so in the beginning there can be these little snips and then these quick repairs, and you can't really tell any damage was done. But when you start paying attention more, the snips are more frequent. Then egocentricity gets in a real bind, because if we continue to pay attention, we are going to see how it all works, how the illusion is created.

The first thing we see is how most of what goes on in our minds is nonsense. Here we are, trying to think deep and yet lofty thoughts, but in fact it's mostly gobbledygook. One of my favorite stories is about the insight Melinda had during a ten-day vipassana retreat. Now, those vipassana meditators are truly dedicated. They sit on the cushion for an hour, walk for an hour, sit for an hour, walk for an hour, from early morning to late at night. So, on the fifth day of this retreat, Melinda was sitting there, having done nothing but meditate day after day, when she heard this plaintive voice in her head: "When am I going to have some time for myself?" That was truly a liberating experience, because she could never again take that voice seriously.

Egocentricity continues to play those tapes that maintain our conditioning. But once you see what is happening, the power of it falls away. You are sitting in meditation, paying attention — snip, snip, snip — seeing through one conditioned belief system after another. And you begin to change; you are not able to hold the identity together in the same way.

Ego's only hope of maintaining the illusion of separateness is to get you to quit paying attention to what goes on in your mind. One good way to do that is to convince you that *this practice is too hard*. We are conditioned to believe that. But if we watch closely, we will see through that belief, too. ◆

The Worthy Opponent

It can sound as if in this practice egocentricity is an enemy, but that is not the case. It is more like Gandhi's seeing his political opponents as teachers: having a worthy opponent is a blessing because it forces you to be your best. In that sense, egocentricity is a blessing.

Sometimes life gets very difficult for people who are working hard at their spiritual practice. That can be confusing, because it seems that instead of supporting their practice, life keeps punishing them, as if they are doing something wrong. But that difficulty can be confirmation of the work that is being done, in that life is providing such challenges, such worthy opponents, to require us to keep coming back to what is best within us.

If we really want to end suffering, it is not helpful to have an easy life, to have things go well in that way that allows us to not pay attention. We tend to believe that an easy life means we are doing it right, because that is the way it worked when we were children. So now if life is punishing us, we think we must be bad.

But we can turn that around and see that each time life gives us that kind of challenge, what we are required to do is come back to being centered, right here, right now, letting go of those ideas of right and wrong, and just being present. If I am looking to the past or future, life can be very difficult, but when I can get right here and now, it is manageable. Every time I come up against adversity, it reminds me that the only place of well-being is right here, right now. ◆

Projection

Here I am with my mass of conditioning, looking out at the world. All of you are my projections. I have no idea at all whether you really exist, and I certainly could not prove that you do. Maybe I am awake and this is all happening in reality, but maybe I am asleep and you are all a dream, and at some point I'll wake up and you'll all be gone. How could I know?

When we talk about projection, people reach a point where they say, "Okay, I'm beginning to see this projection stuff. I project that this person is nice, and I project that that one is a real opportunity" (as we call it). "And I can see that because I know the part of me that is nice, and I know the part of me that is an opportunity. But: what about this other person? We all agree about her, so it is not a projection."

Now, as far as I am concerned, this looking for the "real" truth beyond my projection is not helpful in spiritual practice. It is *all* my projection — everything, everybody, all the time: the good, the bad, and the ugly. It is all mirroring me.

So, where are the boundaries? There aren't any. I cannot keep any of you away from me, because you are all my creations.

Just accepting that is much simpler than trying to figure out what is true. True by whose standards? Who is the "I" who is trying to figure out what is true? Only egocentricity, conditioned mind, the illusion of separateness is interested in answers to such questions. It is so much easier to just allow all those "others" to be embraced within ourselves rather than to be drawing lines to keep them out. ◆

Resistance

Holding an idea of something is resistance, because even an idea of what is, is not what is.

Fear is resistance, and wanting is resistance, and everything except being present in the moment is resistance. The sense of separate self is resistance. "I" am maintained through resistance, through opposition; we have to get on one or the other side of the duality to experience ourselves. Resistance is essential to the ego maintenance system.

Watch the layers of resistance by picking a project and doing it and observing all the resistance that arises. It could be getting through college, or completing a certain job, or having a baby, or bringing up a child, or growing up yourself, or making a commitment — the things people do in life. Listen to yourself say, "I can't do it. It's never going to work."

But if it does work and you are paying close enough attention to see it, then you no longer need to believe that voice. After a while, when resistance arises you simply notice it: "Oh, there is the voice that says it's never going to work." We are conditioned to think that that voice means something is wrong and so we should stop what we are doing. But we can simply acknowledge it — "Oh, that voice again" — and be grateful, because now we have an opportunity to see that what we took to be a limitation is in fact nothing.

Eventually we find out that the only limits are the ones we bring to a situation. And finally those voices stop.

Life will not prove to you that you are inadequate. The only evidence of your inadequacy comes from those voices, that conditioning. If this practice offers one thing to the world, it is the possibility of sitting still through all that fear, all the voices, everything that gets thrown at you by egocentricity — to sit still with an attitude of observing it all and not believing it.

Now: it is helpful to remember not to set up a situation within yourself that would be resisting resistance. ♦

No Control

An idea that has been attributed to the Buddha is that if you lead a good life, good things will follow. What I see in that is the desire for control: we hope that by influencing the cause, we can influence the effect and thereby have control over life.

To me, that is a dangerous notion, because we are the ones who label one part of life good and another part bad. If we think about the *Book of Job*, we may realize that from a spiritual point of view, something could happen to us that we hate with every ounce of our being and yet it could be the best opportunity for our spiritual growth. Now, if we think we are in control, and we are defining what is good and what is bad, we are going to miss out on exactly what might be the most useful experience for us. If I truly want to end the illusion of separateness and the suffering in that, it will not be possible to protect my ego or to keep my spiritual practice within the limits imposed by my conditioning.

Somebody told me how worried they were about the content of their mind, how it was just out of control. But what they were describing was just like my mind, so I wasn't concerned. The first place I encounter lack of control is in my own mind; if I had any control, I would not think about a whole bunch of the things I think about. And I would be present all the time when I meditate. But when we sit down and start looking at our minds, we realize that we cannot control our thoughts. They simply come and go of their own accord.

Likewise, we cannot control our emotions. We might maintain the illusion that we have some control about how we respond to them — except for those times when we seem to have no control over how we respond to them. Then, to preserve this idea that we usually are in control, we say things like "That's just not like me; I don't know what came over me." But, if we look closely, we do not have control over when feelings arise, the form they take, or how we respond to them.

How much control do you have over your body? "Stop hurting, body. Sit still, body."

What do you have control over?

Our conditioning includes amazingly elaborate systems to keep us from facing this simple fact of life: we are not in control. ◆

One Good Reason To Move

When I am asked to advise people who want to pursue spiritual practice but do not live near a teacher, I always say the same thing: move.

Let's say I want to be a ballerina. The only problem is, there are no ballet schools where I live, or any ballet performances, or any ballet dancers. What am I left with? Books on ballet. That's not to say I can't have a heck of a good time in the garage, and once in a while I might make a little trip to New York City and see some great performances and feel very inspired. But if I really want to dance, if I want dancing to be at the center of my life, I will go where people are dancing and where teachers are teaching dancing.

You have about the same chances of doing spiritual practice from a book as doing ballet from a book. You might meditate a lot, but trying to do spiritual practice without a teacher is hard going. It is the same as with anything else: on your own you can learn a certain amount and have a good time and even be a great amateur, but you are unlikely to become proficient.

I wish I had better news. I wish I could say, "Oh, the practice of ending suffering is easy. You'll have it down by next weekend." But it just isn't so. If you want to follow this path, you may need to do something big, like moving to be near a teacher. ♦

The Spiritual Patchwork Quilt

Any awareness is only for that moment. When we try to drag an awareness along to apply somewhere else, we end up creating this bizarre patchwork quilt of awareness. I understand this and I understand that, so I have these two awarenesses, so I'll put them together. And here's this awareness, I could tack it on there — yeah, that looks good — and I have this understanding and, oh, this insight. When I get them all arranged, it becomes my view of the universe, my spiritual package. And now that I've got all these understandings and insights and awarenesses that I can point to, why look any further? That feeling should sound an alarm: we never reach a point where it makes sense to quit looking.

If you have an awareness, that's great — just realize that there's nobody to have it, and there is no place to put it. So, if you are putting it in a framework, you can know you are building a framework of delusion. You see something and realize "Oh, that's it!" — but even the "Oh" is too late. The "Oh" means small mind put it into a framework it can understand, after the fact. That's okay, just don't believe it. Don't try to hold on to realization. ◆

Pain

P_{ain} is a given in life. Suffering is not; suffering is what happens to us when we want something other than what is. Suffering can be anything from feeling irritable or vaguely discontent, all the way to both legs being amputated at the scene of the accident. So, when we talk about suffering, we are not just talking about the horrible things we can experience in life; suffering includes that whole spectrum of wanting something other than what is.

With sitting meditation, pain is something you have to go through at the beginning. It's no different from anything else in life; almost everything has a certain degree of pain associated with it until you get used to it. If I go up to the monastery tomorrow and spend the day working on construction, and the last so many weeks I've spent sitting in a little room talking with people about spiritual practice, then I can expect that after I pound nails all day or carry heavy objects, my muscles will be sore. But if I did that kind of activity every day, pretty soon there would be no pain.

It is simply a matter of what we are accustomed to, how much we put into it, and how much we love doing it. Now, if sitting practice is what you want to do, then you will practice sitting, and your muscles will adapt, just as they do with other activities. Before long, you will develop the ability to sit on the cushion and be comfortable. At a sesshin, almost nobody is sitting in pain, for the simple reason that we all sit a lot. Any suffering happening there does not have to do with the body.

If you allow sitting on the cushion to continue to be physically difficult, it's unlikely that you will develop much of a meditation practice. We just don't seem very attracted to things that make us miserable. (Except relationships: but now we're talking suffering.)

So, if you want to do this practice, I encourage you to sit in meditation posture while you are not meditating. If you are going to read or watch television or talk with a friend, sit on the cushion — you will be able to sit much longer when you are distracted. Before you know it, sitting in meditation for half an hour will be a piece of cake. ♦

The Myth of an Alternative Reality

It is possible for me to imagine things that are not. For example, I can imagine that I should be wealthy. I know wealthy people, I know how they live, I know how their houses look. I should be one of them. I should not be living this impoverished life that I am living; I know my real life is as a rich person. Or, I can imagine that in a certain situation, if I had said such and such, then this other person would have said such and such, and we would have felt this way, and we would have done that, and then I would have been happy. But since none of that happened, clearly I made a mistake.

Now, we can do that kind of imagining about everything. We can always imagine a reality we prefer to the one we are actually living, so that this world always comes out short. The trees aren't tall enough; the water isn't blue enough; there is only one rainbow.

If we acknowledge that such wishful thinking exists nowhere but in our imagination and we simply drop it, then there is no reality but what is right here, there is nothing but *this*. We can say that this is an evil and hideous place, or we can say that this is a perfect place. Or we could say nothing. Where we get into trouble is when we say some things are good and some things are bad, this is the right way and that is the wrong way. In fact, this is the only world we have, this is the only moment that is, and we can call it perfect, imperfect, nothing — it doesn't matter. It simply is as it is. There is no alternative.

Now, that says nothing about the next moment. But there's a little trick here, in that this moment is all that exists. ♦

The Ideal Relationship

From a spiritual point of view, the ideal relationship is the one you are in, because the relationship you are really dealing with is always the relationship with yourself.

A relationship will bring out the very worst in you, and that is what makes it your best opportunity to find the best in you. Seeing the worst forces you to find the best — or pack the car. And down deep you know that packing the car is a waste of time; you will just unpack it somewhere else and go through the same thing all over again. So, at some point, take a stand: I am going to go through it right here.

You come together with another person because you are attracted to aspects of each other, you feel better with each other. Then that phase of the relationship passes, and you are left with the fact that the other person is no longer mirroring you in the way that makes you feel good about yourself. And whose fault is it? Theirs, of course; in fact, you can easily point out any number of things they do that are starting to ruin the great thing you had going. But blaming the other person is like getting angry at the mirror because you don't look the way you want to look.

It is important to get beyond blame, not because blaming is wrong, but because for your own well-being you choose not to leave your own inner peace; it is not worth it to blame somebody else if the price you pay is the misery of being filled with anger or hatred or vengefulness. When you catch yourself ready to blame, ask yourself this. Do I really want to be upset over this? Am I willing to suffer over this? Is it going to feel so good to yell at somebody that I am willing to sacrifice my own peace and accept the consequences of my anger?

And when I have just yelled and blamed, do I then hate myself for it? No.

If all else fails, meditate. If you cannot quit yelling and blaming or whatever it is, go meditate any time you feel that arising. If it is your intention to stay with that internal experience of goodness, and something is keeping you from it, go sit on the cushion until it passes.

Some of you, no doubt, will fear that you might spend the rest of your life on the cushion. Well, is that so bad? Why not just risk it? If the alternative is continuing with a life of anger and blame and resentment, I would be in favor of taking the chance.

Sitting on the cushion is the best way to be with yourself. In meditation you examine exactly what is happening, you cultivate a relationship with your own heart. And that is the only relationship that matters. ◆

Spiritual Correctness

Discussions of harmlessness often lead to questions like, where do you draw the line about what life forms you do and do not kill?

Within myself, it is not necessary to draw any lines, because I am always responding to an internal sense of how something feels to me. Obviously I eat. People will ask me, "What about a carrot? Don't you think a carrot feels?" Maybe it does. However, looking into the eyes of a carrot and looking into the eyes of a cow, I have a very different experience, such that right now I am going to eat the carrot, and I am not going to eat the cow. I would ask people who can eat cows with no difficulty to spend a little time looking in the eyes of a cow and see if it seems like there is anybody home there.

It is not compassionate to *this* creature [pointing to self] not to eat anything at all — nor would it be compassionate to force myself to eat the cow.

People argue that because the nervous system of a mosquito is not developed to the point that it can understand itself as a separate being, it's okay to kill them. When I look at a mosquito, though, I clearly see that it is alive, and it is going about its life. Just because I cannot see into its eyes does not mean it doesn't have eyes, it just means my seeing is too gross. Why should the mosquito pay with its life for the limitations of my perception?

It is also argued that if you are three times removed from the killing of a creature, it's okay to eat it. That means if somebody kills it and somebody else processes it and somebody else sells it, there is no harm in buying it and eating it. The word "rationalization" always springs to my mind when I hear that. Why would people go to the trouble to rationalize something like that if they did not in their heart suspect that it wasn't the thing to do?

I go so far as to not eat with people who are eating creatures. When this peculiarity of mine is mentioned, I am sometimes asked how I avoid offending people. The answer is, if I lived my life to avoid offending people, I'd be out of a job. But usually I am not in situations where this is a difficulty. I arrange it that way; I do not lead retreats where anything other than vegetarian food is served, because I cannot look at the flesh and not think about the creature.

I am not suggesting any "shoulds" based on a notion that not eating meat is the more spiritual thing to do. In fact, "the more spiritual thing to do" is an idea that is always interesting to question. ◆

Correctness and Compassion

When I came out of the monastery, I lived awhile with an elderly woman, and I ended up taking care of her as she was dying. And she wanted to eat meat.

What to do? Lecture her on the evils of consuming the flesh of other creatures and the bad karma of said activity? Or try to see, in the moment, what is the most compassionate for all?

Maybe the most compassionate thing would have been to deliver an enlightened discourse to this woman, who would have had her eyes opened to universal truth and ascended immediately into nirvana. Instead, I fried a chicken for her. Knowing that I could be totally wrong, and being willing to live with that possibility. ◆

Ah. Hm.

Recently a woman came to see me with a difficulty in her life, which was that she was starting an affair with her husband's best friend. She wanted me to take a position, but my response was the only one I can imagine: "Hm. Yeah. Ah. No kidding." And there's always "Wow." I keep that right at the forefront of my arsenal of clever Zen responses. I mean this sincerely, in the sense of "Yes, I know what that's like. A truly fine spiritual opportunity."

What else is there to say? We talked about how she expected me to tell her that what she was doing was wrong and she should stop, and how she would then go ahead and do it anyway because nobody was going to tell her what was right for her. But because I did not tell her what to do, she was left with what *she* believes about it. There was no encouragement for her to do or not do anything. She got to hear her story, and that experience was like a mirror in which she could see herself in this situation.

When I was growing up my mother had this clipping taped inside the door of the kitchen cupboard so you saw it every time you got out a glass. It said, "Do not despair that you cannot make others as you would wish them to be, since you cannot make yourself as you would wish to be." So, until I have my own failings and weaknesses firmly in the far distant past, I feel I am not in a position to offer much to people about theirs other than "Hm" or "Wow" or "Is that so?" So, my job is actually quite easy.

I work with a lot of people who say they are confused. As quickly and as gently as possible, I ask them to consider that they are not confused at all, but that they have a belief system that says, "If I know what I am doing and how I should be reacting, and if I don't do the right thing, then I'm a bad person."

Let's say you know you need to end a marriage to someone who is beating your children. But you are terrified to confront that issue, for a thousand reasons, so you get confused. As long as you are in that state, it's not your fault you are not making any movement, because you don't know what you should be doing, you're trying so hard but you just can't figure it out . . . on and on. That state of confusion feels like a safe place to be.

I encourage people in that situation to consider that it is all right to be exactly where they are, to understand exactly what is going on, and to do nothing — to simply say, "This is where I am, and I'm afraid to make a move." What is wrong with that? ◆

A Secret
of the Universe

If you suspect that you are perpetuating a habit pattern in order to protect yourself from another experience — for example, getting confused to avoid looking honestly at a situation — don't use that against yourself. See if you can go right ahead doing exactly what you are doing, with the attitude that you know nothing, not assuming that there is a better way to be. Pay really close attention, and you will learn a lot.

It's hard to do, isn't it? You catch on to something, you know you are doing something you don't approve of, you know you are not supposed to disapprove of it. You are trying really hard to be all right with yourself and not beat yourself up for how you are, but you desperately want to be different.

My recommendation is, just watch it. It may take several dozen times, a hundred times, five hundred times of doing the same thing before you actually see what is going on. It may be easier if we realize that we have been doing these same things for eons, so we can do them a few more times.

Here is a little item to jot down in your notebook under

Secrets of the Universe. You only have to experience a conditioned response pattern once with your heart and mind completely open, and that pattern will be finished forever.

There is nothing in that statement about changing or being different or letting go or getting rid of anything. The moment you are absolutely present to whatever it is, it is finished. And if it's not, you won't care a bit. ◆

Happiness

Many people have the idea that doing spiritual practice or being a spiritual person means that everything is wonderful and peaceful and joyful. We think that being happy is everything, that when the tablets came down from the mountain, what they actually said was, Thou shalt be happy no matter what. Being miserable, being stuck, doesn't fit with our idea of a spiritual person.

I know a lot about this subject, because being a spiritual teacher, I am expected to be happy. If I'm not, people take that as a sign that this practice doesn't work.

It is very difficult to let go of the idea that we will at some point have some sort of experience, an awakening, that will leave us happy forever. If that were true, it would be good for business, but in fact this practice will never make a lot of money because we are not selling the right thing. There is no promise of life eternal. (Oh, we could promise it, but an endless round of reincarnations is not what people have in mind when they hear that term.) There is nothing in this practice that anybody would want to buy. It is not going to get you anything; it is not going to make you any different. And people don't want to hear that. Why do a spiritual practice, then? If I'm not going to be happy, why bother?

Another popular misunderstanding of the spiritual path is the opposite, that it involves deprivation and self-denial. But that is definitely not what the Buddha taught. Often, in fact, it is harder to let go and receive than to let go and deprive ourselves. Letting go and not having something seems so spiritual. But can we let go of that idea as well? Can we let go and be happy when we're happy, be sad when we're sad, be upset when we're upset, be lonely when we're lonely, be frightened when we're frightened? Can we simply be whatever it is without needing to be someone who is having that experience? Can each experience simply happen and that be all right? Otherwise, aren't we letting go of happiness and grabbing on to deprivation — becoming a person who is deprived, then perceiving ourselves as spiritual because of that? When you put those two together, it can be deadly; if you require yourself to be happy and devote yourself to deprivation, you meet yourself coming and going.

The Zen monk Ryokan wrote about what it was like to be out there in his hut in the dead of winter: it was cold, and he was lonely. This upset people, because it didn't match their image of a Zen master. And yet he was simply experiencing what he was experiencing, being completely present to his life, not grasping after somebody else's idea of what his life should be like.

It is a trap to believe that if I am not happy, there is something wrong with my spiritual practice. Egocentricity can use that belief to keep us from pursuing a spiritual practice, because as soon as we encounter something that makes us unhappy, we won't want to do it. If we believe that every time we are unhappy, we must not be doing spiritual practice right, ego really has us in its grip.

But trying to get rid of this idea will not work. The more helpful attitude is to allow it to be there, but without believing it. Pay attention; observe all the ways that you hold this notion that if you are a good person, you will be happy. Let that idea arise without resisting it, until it just doesn't arise anymore.

Anger is a good example. We think being angry is not spiritual, but in fact, it is important to be angry until you don't need to anymore. In this duality of good person/bad person, doing spiritual practice/not doing spiritual practice, we are afraid to be angry. Yet we have been doing these same things — being angry, being harsh with ourselves, exacting punishment on ourselves and others — forever. And we can risk doing them for a few more months or years in this lifetime, opening ourselves again and again to the experience, until we reach the point of no longer needing to do them.

Embracing the unhappiness takes the wind out of its sails. Once it is as okay to be unhappy as to be happy, there is no more charge to it. At that point, we are truly free. ♦

"It's God's Will" Versus "Thy Will Be Done"

These two expressions have very different meanings to me. Calling something God's will sounds as if that is all there is to say about it, that's the end of it, that's that. But life doesn't stop there.

Once at the monastery a tree fell across the road, and cars could not pass. Somebody said it was God's will. But if you stop with that, no one can ever come or go. Now what? Now go get the chainsaw and cut the tree up and clear the road.

Of course, then we could say that clearing the road is God's will. We can say anything is God's will — which is all right, except for the idea that something is finished, signed and sealed, so we can forget about it, we don't have to pay attention.

"Thy will be done," on the other hand, has for me a feeling of the miracle of everything happening every moment. All that is required of me is to get out of the way and not interfere with it. "It's God's will" leaves me having to figure out what is God's will and what isn't God's will, whereas "Thy will be done" has the sense of what is, is. It's like living: life is happening, and there is nothing to figure out about it. It is not as if one thing is and another thing is not, one thing belongs to life and another doesn't. It all just *is*.

I often turn to Christian sayings about God because Buddhism doesn't have any. Buddhists say things like "From the beginning, no thing is." It's true, but it's a little hard to get a grip on. And that's the point, of course, because spiritual practice is not about getting a better grip on things. But something like "Thy will be done" can be a tool we use to reach a certain perspective. When we reach that perspective, we can put the tool down. In Buddhism we say you use a raft to cross to the other shore, but on the other side, you leave the raft behind. The raft is useful only for crossing the water; once you have reached dry land, it doesn't help any more. So when you reach an understanding of "Thy will be done," then you can drop it.

At that point, you might want to take up something like "From the beginning, no thing is." But if you turn that into a belief system — something to relate to so you can know you are a person who understands that from the beginning no thing is — then you're back to trying to paddle that raft across dry land.

As for who "Thy" refers to, we Buddhists do not even speculate about that. It is true that some Buddhists refer to something that sounds an awful lot like God. In Jiyu Kennett's books, for example, there is frequent mention of the "Lord of the House." This sets a lot of people on edge, because in this culture, practically everybody who is Buddhist is a convert, and when you convert from the Judeo-Christian background to Buddhism and run into the "Lord of the House," you might wonder if you have made any progress. And yet Jiyu Kennett is using those words to point to something quite different from what the words usually mean. If you look carefully at her writings and those of some other teachers, you can get a sense that they are talking about something, but only in the most negative of ways; they are talking about something that is not, instead of something that is. And yet you are not left with the impression that they are talking about nothing.

In other words, when you come across a reference to "Buddha-nature," what does this mean? If you are a Christian, you might say it means Christ-consciousness or God. The danger in that, from the Buddhist perspective, is that if you develop too much of a relationship with these kinds of concepts, you may start thinking you know something, that you have the truth about something. And then belief systems are formed.

One of the most fundamental perspectives of Buddhism is "Form is emptiness, emptiness is form." Now, to try to build a belief system around that simply is not helpful.

At the same time, would we be sitting here doing this if we were not having some sort of experience of what that means?

All this talk we do, trying to see how everything fits together, is to get to the realization that form is emptiness and emptiness is form. We simply take belief systems apart and take them apart and take them apart until there is nothing left. Of course, while we are busy taking one apart over here, we are busy building up another one over there; we simply take all the pieces of this structure and recombine them to create another one, and then we will tear that one apart, and we could do this forever. If we don't have a meditation practice, we could be going around in circles, lost in the psychological stuff, moving pieces around, trying to figure it out —

small mind trying to figure out how all this goes together. What we are really trying to figure out, however, is not how all this stuff goes together, but how it can come apart.

What happens to a person when it begins to come apart, when you begin to see your identity fall away? There is no place to get a firm footing; everything you try to hold on to just slips through your fingers. You are able to let go of the belief systems, of everything you held on to, only if you have what this practice gives you: the ability to come back to the moment, to come back to the breath and to the peace and joy and comfort that is there.

"Thy will be done" was of utmost comfort to me in that process of identity beginning to fall away. I did not need to figure it out, I did not need to make a decision about it, there was nothing for me to do. It was simply possible to be present and say, "Yes. Thy will be done." That is what those words mean to me. I did not need to know whose will or why or what would happen next. My job was simply to say yes. ♦

Work Out
Your Own Salvation
Diligently

At the moment of death, somebody else's enlightenment is going to be of no help to us. The only thing we take with us is what is available to us in that moment. So it is imperative that we not worry about what anybody else is doing, not compare ourselves to anyone else, or imagine how we ourselves might be at some future point. Instead, we should devote all our time and energy and attention and effort to being as present as we can in this moment.

People project their innocence, their goodness, their holiness onto someone else — a spiritual teacher, for example — hoping that person will embody those qualities and reflect them back. That has been going on for as long as there have been people, and so has the abuse of that. Every time some melodrama erupts in a spiritual center, people get disillusioned and say, "See, there's nothing good in this world, nobody you can believe in, nobody you can count on." Why don't we simply drop that foolish idea? Wouldn't that be a lot easier? If each of us takes responsibility for our own spiritual practice, then we wouldn't have to be disillusioned. I think our compassion for one another would grow dramatically if we would simply look to ourselves, trust that we are doing the best we can, realizing that when we see how we can do better, we will do better. It doesn't matter what anybody else is doing! It doesn't matter how good they are, how bad they are, how moral, how immoral.

The Buddha is a great model of taking responsibility for one's own spiritual training. He went around seeking out teacher after teacher, and he learned from each one. After those experiences, he still was not satisfied, because no one seemed to know the answers to the questions he was asking. So he said, "I guess it's up to me. I may not succeed, but at least I'll give it my best effort." Fortunately for us, he was quite successful. But the fact that he was successful doesn't mean we don't have to do it for ourselves. He showed us that it can be done, and he left us a lot of guidance about how it is done, but he couldn't do it for us. It's still up to us. In fact, the Buddha's last instructions to his students were *Work out your own salvation diligently.*

No one else can do it for you. No one else can save you. The wonder of it is that we are required to *become* that which will save us. ♦

Being Stuck and Sticking It Out

There's the Garden of Eden, which we hear about as a highly desirable possibility, and then there's this hell of our own lives. The central question of spiritual practice is, how do we get from here to there?

In Buddhism we say there is nowhere to go. The Garden of Eden is right here. So is hell. There is no difference between them; nirvana and samsara are one. But when you've been cast out into the weeping-and-wailing-and-gnashing-of-teeth club, hearing how nirvana and samsara are one just isn't much consolation.

Last year I was as depressed as I've ever been, and I've been pretty depressed. With years of spiritual practice, with the psychological tools at my disposal, all the tricks of the trade — plus just having published a book on depression as a spiritual opportunity — I was still depressed. What I found out was, there's nothing to do. And you know, it's not so bad. If your energy level is reduced to a hundredth of what it was, extremely small elevations in mood become very significant. You just live with it. You even enjoy it.

When it comes to being stuck, it doesn't matter who you

listen to — St. Teresa of Avila, Krishnamurti, Gautama Buddha, or just about anybody who has made a sincere effort at doing a spiritual practice — they will tell you about the same pitfalls, and the same way out. Basically, there are two kinds of pitfalls. Being out-and-out stuck is when you think you cannot go on. (Some people are convinced they will die; one man told me he had such panic attacks before retreats that he knew he would be killed on the way to the retreat center.) "Dry spells" are when you are just uninspired. No demons or devils; you'd be grateful for something terrible, something to struggle with, but it is just the same old boring sitting down on your cushion and falling asleep, sit down, fall asleep. There can be months of that, when you feel nothing.

In either case, if you stay with it, you will learn the most important lesson in life — a very famous lesson, delivered by a non-Buddhist — which is "This, too, shall pass." And the critical realization for us is, of course, that this life shall pass.

So, with each moment, no matter what is going on, the practice is to find the willingness, the courage, the faith, the compassion simply to come back to the present, come back to this heart, come back to this person — not to give up just because it's difficult. For me, an equivalent of willingness is grace: the great blessing that within being stuck, there is a little moment of clarity, of knowing that something else is possible. When we open ourselves to that knowledge, that is willingness. ♦

ALREADY ENLIGHTENED

Inherent Goodness

In practicing meditation, we grow daily more accustomed to spaciousness, to a feeling of freedom. We begin to associate that experience with peace, with joy, with well-being, rather than with loss of identity and fear. So we practice coming back to the present, dropping everything and coming back again and again and again, and we realize that nothing happens to us; we are perfectly fine. When we are sitting quietly in meditation and all of the other stuff falls away, what is left is goodness.

If you are ever going to be free, you must be willing to prove to yourself that your true nature is inherent goodness — that when you stop doing everything else, goodness is what is there. You will never prove it to yourself as long as you believe the egocentric conditioning that says the only thing making you a good person is your inner judging and punishing and beating yourself, in all the ways we do that. You must find the courage to stop judging and punishing yourself long enough to find out that who you are is goodness. ♦

The Centered Place

To me, all this psychological-sounding discussion is wonderfully helpful, because that's how my mind works. I like to have a picture of things; if I'm going to do something, I like to know how it fits in with everything else.

Psychological insight, however, is useless, as far as I can tell, without sitting meditation. But sitting practice is not useless without psychological insight. You could sit down facing a wall, and eventually you would see everything.

Of course, hardly anybody is willing to just sit there until they see it all. What most people aim for is an intellectual understanding of this practice. But that is like having an intellectual understanding of riding a bicycle. It's great when you are sitting in the living room looking at the instruction book, but when you're flying down a hill on the bicycle, it doesn't help. The only thing that is helpful is actual practice.

In meditation we find that deep sense of well-being within ourselves, that inherent goodness, and we become friends with that. We learn how to embrace our daily life within our spiritual practice by bringing troubling events into that still place where there is peace, into that circle of compassion and acceptance. We discover that when we are in that centered place, all problems dissolve.

Then we get caught up again, our minds take off, we get lost in our conditioned reactions, but then again we bring our attention back. We practice that coming back here, to the present moment, to our heart. Then we go out and get miserable, then we come back again. There is going out and getting miserable, and then there is coming back here. Eventually I see "here" as a place of compassion and "out there" as a place of suffering — and there is just no comparison. I simply do not want to be out there any more. I'm not pushing anything away, it's just that I see what is going on, and I want to come back here.

It's good not to wait until you are in crisis to try this. When you are in crisis, the important thing is to survive it. Then when things have settled down, you can begin to find that place of compassion and spend more time there, developing the relationship with your own heart, or however you talk about it. Practice it when everything is fine, and then when something goes wrong, that experience is there for you. Coming back to the centered place becomes automatic; it becomes the foundation for your life. ♦

Getting Impersonal

One thing I like about practicing with a group is that we begin to see how impersonal it all is — all our melodramas that can seem so terribly personal. If we spent six months together, we all would know each other's life stories, and it would be the same story. One person lives in Toledo, another one lives in Shanghai, but it is the same story. Being a human being is pretty much the same for all of us; the differences are far, far less than the similarities. What we think, what we fear, how our emotions arise — fundamentally, we are very much alike. We get caught up in differences in content because that is how we experience ourselves as separate.

Working in a group enables us to see not only how we are all attached to the same things, but how, when we are attached, we suffer, and how, when we come back to the present moment, we cease to suffer. It's that straightforward.

As we see the sameness of our experience, our suffering becomes less charged: our story is one more story among countless stories. It becomes easier to find the courage to bring our attention back to the present, to allow whatever happens simply to happen and not take it personally, to know that it has nothing to do with anything but conditioning, and it has been this way since before the beginning of beginningless time. Then the attachment, the illusion, the suffering begins to fall away. ◆

Being Helpful

We never get a guarantee that what we are doing will be helpful.

There is a story about an old holy man who meditated every morning on the banks of the Ganges. One morning he saw a scorpion that had been swept away by the river's current and was in danger of drowning. The old man reached out to rescue the scorpion, but the scorpion stung his hand. The man tried again, but each time he touched the scorpion, it stung him. This went on for some time, and the man's hand became swollen and bloodied. A passerby asked the old man why he persisted in something that caused him injury, and for the sake of such a worthless creature. The old man answered, "Just because it is the nature of the scorpion to sting doesn't mean I should give up my nature, which is to help."

It is disconcerting to try to save an insect, say, from a spider, and find that what you have done is help it out of one of its legs or wings. And yet it does seem to be our nature to be moved to sympathy. It may be projecting from our own suffering, but I think that's how we find most of our compassion. We simply do the best we can, and we never know what the result will be.

One of the things I like best about Buddhism is that there are not any answers. There is no handbook that says, in case of this, do that. You just have to sit still with each experience; one time it might feel right to do something, another time it might not.

I always take care of myself, letting that be what motivates me, because within the idea of letting things be as they are, I have to include letting myself be the way I am. ♦

Innocence

We have the idea that we must watch out so we will not be taken advantage of. But spiritually speaking, if the choice is between taking advantage and being taken advantage of, I would rather be in the second camp. If I am a little innocent, if out of my sincere hoping and trusting for the best there is, I am on the gullible side — surely worse things could happen. I would rather be that than be hard and cold and jaded and cynical and calculating. To open up your heart and risk being naive or even foolish — that is what Jesus meant when he said we should "become as little children." That innocent, trusting openness is the mind and heart of spiritual life.

One of the things that is so charming about children is that they know they are powerless; they know they have no choices, so they are defenseless. It is only when we start believing in our own power and feeling we are in charge that we need to protect ourselves, that we need to be cautious and smart. And then we lose the innocence.

If you are going along with an open innocent heart, and you

make a mistake (which I don't consider possible), then it's just a learning experience. Not learning not to make that "mistake" again, but learning not to be hard on yourself about it. What could you do in innocence that you would want to learn not to do again? Not trust someone? Not believe people? Not be open?

One of the notions that is most helpful to me is that truth has no application. There is nothing we can learn that will help us in the next moment. Whenever I say that, somebody inevitably describes a truth that does have application later, like learning to wear an ankle brace when you run after you've injured an ankle. But what I am talking about is wearing that ankle brace the rest of your life. And getting one for the other ankle. And giving one to everybody you know.

By the time we are adults, so much of what we believe, what we are operating from, is like that ankle brace: it has nothing to do with our lives now. We are still protecting ourselves — as if there were a self to protect. The Buddha taught that the separate self is an illusion, it doesn't exist. So, we are attempting to support something that isn't, to protect something that isn't, to maintain something that isn't. It's an awful lot of effort for something that isn't.

This practice dissolves the notion of something separate that must be maintained and defended, so that we can simply be the openness and innocence that is our true nature. ◆

Loving the Ego Out of Existence

To me, it's awe-inspiring to think of someone like the Buddha. What an extraordinary effort: to continue to come back to being fully present in spite of everything, to face all the voices, all the beliefs, all the fears. Most of us are not willing to do that. And so we want to think of the Buddha as a magical person, endowed in ways that we are not.

But we have everything that is necessary to do the same thing, to awaken. It is also true that it is very hard to stay with it, unless there is somebody pushing us. The good news is that probably everybody who undertakes sitting practice has that person pushing them — from the inside. Not as fast as the Buddha, perhaps, but that's okay.

Sometimes we get the feeling that we will never be quite clever enough or quick enough to see through it all — the layers of conditioning, the illusions thrown up by egocentricity. And that is the reason for meditation. Meditation is the one thing you have in your repertoire that egocentricity does not have. When you bring your attention back here, when you drop everything and come back to the breath, egocentricity has no defense against that. It can do anything and everything to try to keep you from returning to that centered place, but once you do it, that's it for egocentricity. It just dissolves.

I am not talking about killing the ego, I am not talking about a violent process, so "dissolving the ego" may be an unfortunate choice of words. I hope you are not envisioning something like pouring acid on the ego or any other harmful or destructive means. The ego is not evil; it is an inescapable product of human conditioning. To define it as the enemy and want to destroy it would defeat the whole purpose of this practice; it would be contrary to the gentleness and goodness and wholeness we are trying to acknowledge in ourselves.

What I am talking about is loving the ego out of existence, loving it into being a non-issue. What I am talking about is nothing more than ending suffering. It is finding the strength and courage to bring in those parts of oneself that are afraid and hurt and angry and deprived and to embrace them and accept them. It is taking all the wounded and suffering beings within oneself and drawing them into that circle of compassion so they can be reassured and healed and comforted. Because, in our hearts, we know that all that suffering is not necessary. ♦

Commitment

Once you make a commitment, anything is possible. Now, this is not how we ordinarily see it. But this practice asks us to question our usual assumptions. So, consider this. Until you make a commitment, you waffle: "Well, I don't know; maybe I won't feel like it next week." As long as there is a back door, you will be glancing at it and thinking about escape, and you won't look in the direction of freedom. You won't let go, because you are convinced that what you are holding on to will be enough for you.

But it is not enough.

The only thing that will ever be enough is what you have within yourself, the freedom that exists within your own heart and mind. The only way to prove that to yourself is to let go of everything. Until you have that experience, you will not accept that your true nature lies in that inherent goodness, that compassion, that peace inside. You will not turn to that internal experience as long as you have something else that you are holding on to.

But once you make a commitment, you have nothing to lose, because you have given up worrying about whether you will like it later or what will happen if you change your mind. Changing your mind is no longer an option. Now you have no back door, no escape. Whatever arises, you will face it, you will deal with it, you will embrace it. You will let go and find freedom within whatever happens. ♦

The Special Experience

Most of us believe there is a special experience other people have that we do not have. That belief keeps egocentricity firmly in charge, because no matter what experience you do have, the voice of egocentricity can say, "No, that wasn't it; that wasn't the special experience."

Notice what often happens: you bring your attention to the moment, and there is a welling up. You interpret that as, say, sadness, and then you are off thinking about how you wish you lived more in the moment, you've missed so much of your life not being in the moment, and if only you had been more in the moment when — whatever. But none of that is necessary. The constant focus on "Is this it? Am I really centered? Am I in the moment now? Am I having the right spiritual experience?" takes us away from the moment. If we were present to the moment, those questions would not arise. Whenever you hear yourself ask, "Am I centered now?" the answer is no.

How will you know if you are centered? You won't know. Then why do this? Why pursue a spiritual practice if you cannot get a guarantee that you are going to do it right, if you cannot know when you are enlightened?

In fact, you already are enlightened. The only reason you do not experience that is because it is egocentricity that is trying to know that it is enlightened. But egocentricity will never be enlightened.

So what is the answer? Just do your practice; just bring your attention back to the present, back to the breath. "Am I doing it right?" Just come back to the breath. "This is not getting me anywhere." Just come back to the breath. "Is this the special experience?" Just come back to the breath. Something in you wants to know if you are enlightened. Just come back to the breath.

When we ask, "Is this it?" the answer is no, for the simple reason that by the time you ask that question, you are no longer present. You will never find an explanation for what "it" is. But what we can see is the egocentric attachment to wanting to know; what we can experience most clearly is what enlightenment is not.

That is why Buddhism often expresses things in the negative. What are we looking for? Some religions say God, but Buddhism does not, because that implies something other than God that is seeking; it makes what we are seeking into a *this* as opposed to *that*. And it's not a this or a that. We get an idea of it, we conceptualize it, then we can say we know what it is — but "I" can never know what it is, because "I" refers to the experience of being separate. Volumes are written about how you cannot say anything about what it is that we are seeking.

My teacher liked to say that some people consider it a miracle to walk on water, but he considers it a miracle to walk on the earth.

Even a moment of clarity is a miracle. If I am sitting in meditation and my attention wanders, it is a miracle that I bring it back to the present. It is a miracle that I am sitting here and that I have the willingness to commit to a spiritual practice.

If you want to have a special experience, just be alive in this moment. Being present to all that is — that is the truly extraordinary experience. ♦

Grace Is When We Say Yes

It seems to me that grace is nothing more than letting go completely. When an opportunity arises to let go of conditioning and be with what is going on in the present moment, and we accept that opportunity with no resistance, the whole world opens up in front of us, like the parting of the Red Sea. Obstacles disappear; suddenly there's enough time, there's money, there's energy, people are agreeable, things fall into place. Life feels magical. God is not only on our side but holding our hand and smiling on everything we attempt to do. It's just yes, yes, yes, yes, yes.

But when we look closely, the experience of being completely present is no different from any other, except that while the rest of life is saying yes, for a change we are not saying no. For that little period of time, what we are getting and what we want are the same.

That may sound passive, as if life is just happening, but when we are in the experience, it doesn't feel passive at all. It's exciting; there is a sense of eager participation. We are open and available. So, to say that what we want and what we get are the same simply means that we are saying yes to what is. ◆

Service

The Zen monk Ryokan lived as a hermit, and according to his poems, the way he spent his life was to go down to the village and play with the children during the day and then go way back in the woods and be by himself. And there are others we know of in the Zen tradition who, like Ryokan, did not devote themselves to good works, who were not involved in fixing things. That is perfectly in keeping with Zen; Zen is not a practice of service in that way.

There is, of course, the bodhisattva vow, which is not to enter nirvana until all beings have awakened, but that is not the same as doing good works. The bodhisattva vow does not require you to rush around to pick people up and drag them to nirvana at great personal cost to yourself.

For me, there is no such thing as service, the way that term is usually meant. The idea that we can do something for somebody else requires that we draw a boundary between ourselves and the other person so there is someone separate to receive our help. In that way, the idea that I am serving you perpetuates egocentricity.

In fact, all I am ever doing is my own spiritual training. For me, spiritual practice is service. If it takes the form of doing something that in some specific way affects someone else, and I define that as "service," fine.

Where we get into trouble is making that fundamental split between me and you. When I make that division, when I experience you as separate from me, then there is the illusion that I can do something for you that is different from doing for me. The problem with that approach is that if I am doing something for you, I am going to want something back from you, whether it's thanks or an acknowledgement that you appreciate what I have done or a certain response — I am going to want you to do something you may not do. But if I am simply living and I understand that living is service, living is giving, because there is nothing that can happen to you that does not happen to me and nothing can happen to me that does not happen to you, then nobody owes anybody anything. We are all simply doing what we feel moved to do.

Now, if we have not taken care of ourselves first, then we are acting out of need, and needy people can never be truly helpful because they come into a situation trying to get something.

But that is not to say we should postpone service until we have completely resolved our problems. I am suggesting that service is more honest if it springs from wanting to be helpful, because feeling helpful furthers our own spiritual growth. We want to do this for ourselves, not because anybody lacks anything we are going to provide.

As long as we believe people need something from us, that there are things we need to fix out there, we don't have to find that experience of need right here within ourselves. We are busy trying to fix this and that and the other thing. Maybe we are being helpful, maybe not.

But when we know that what we are attempting to do is end the suffering within ourselves, at least our effort will result in some piece of suffering being finished with. And the clearer it gets here within ourselves, the more possible it is to be truly helpful out there.

It is not my experience that we are here to fix the world, that we are here to change anything at all. I think we are here so the world can change us. And if part of that change is that the suffering of the world moves us to compassion, to awareness, to sympathy, to love, that is a very good thing. But if we move away from such experience within ourselves in an effort to fix something "out there," we probably lose our best opportunity. We need to remember that as long as there is an "in here" that needs something, there will be an "out there" that needs something. ◆

Simplicity

When we begin paying attention to our minds, so much is going on that it can seem very complex. But we are always dealing with the same thing: our attention is here, in the present, with whatever is happening, or it is somewhere else. Here or there. That's all that's ever going on, in all those situations that arise and seem so important to us and make things look so complicated.

What takes us everywhere else, away from the present, is our conditioning. But all we need to do is let go of whatever it is that takes our attention away and come back to the present. We get into all this mental complexity just because it is such a deeply ingrained habit. There is nothing that says we have to do that.

If I say that all you need to do is drop everything and bring your attention back to the breath, that sounds impossibly simple. "What about this? How could I deal with that?" But those questions are just more of the moving away from being present. The more you are able to stay centered, to keep your attention focused right here, the simpler things become. ◆

At the End
of the Rainbow

Much of this practice has to do with becoming the kind, loving, attentive person you always wanted in your life but never had. We begin to let go of the wish that love will come from somebody other than ourselves — mother, father, spouse, lover, whoever. We begin to realize that we are not going to find anybody else to turn to, to hold us. It is very hard to give up the belief that at the end of the rainbow there will be somebody with their arms open for us. And when we do let go of that wish, there is sadness in it, there is grieving.

I suspect, however, that this wish will turn out to be fulfilled. At the end of the rainbow there *will* be somebody — somebody you never imagined, because to the conditioned mind, which sees the self as separate and therefore insufficient, this somebody is simply inconceivable.

Who is it? The person at the end of the rainbow is yourself, and the experience you seek exists within your own heart and nowhere else. If that experience were not already a part of you, it would never occur to you to look for it. It is just that we are conditioned to look outside ourselves rather than within. What you seek is the deepest part of yourself, which you have felt separate from and longed for and will finally come home to. It is what causes you to seek the truth and peace and love that in your heart you have always known is possible.

Only when we are ready to grieve over the loss of our hope that somebody else will be there for us can we be open to the possibility of what actually *is* there. That is why I nudge people on to be willing to grow up, to take responsibility for themselves. Parts of us want to remain children and have someone else take care of us, someone else who is right and perfect and good. If we could be embraced in the goodness of that other person, and be safe and happy forever, then we wouldn't have to be right and perfect and good ourselves.

It takes some of us quite a lot of paying close attention before we are ready to say, "Okay, that was a wonderful dream, but now it's time to get on with life." But once we say that, our dream *can* come true. The treasure is right there at the end of the rainbow after all, just waiting for us to discover it.

It is not my experience that in spiritual practice we give up ourselves. It is a process of finding ourselves. Not the small, fearful, isolated, constricted mass of conditioned suffering — it is true that we are required to give that up. But it is replaced by who you really are, your true nature, which is freedom and bliss and joy.

It is an incredibly good trade. ◆

Free Fall

I would offer you this to consider: the only thing that fears is egocentricity. The only thing that anything can happen to is egocentricity. So, trying to protect the ego from experiences it does not want to have will not work. The ego is not going to be ready for any of the experiences it will have in spiritual practice. Waiting for it to get ready is a colossal waste of time.

In this practice, everything I ever thought was true slides right out of my grasping, clinging fingers. Everything I ever hoped would be so, everything I ever believed in slips away. What am I left with? Nothing. Nothing to hold on to. Nowhere to stand. Nowhere to be.

That can be terrifying or liberating, depending on your point of view. In my experience, if I am lost in my conditioning, it is terrifying. If I am right here, centered, fully present, it is liberating. ◆

Only Good Begets Good

No spiritual benefit will ever come from anything other than love; nothing good can come from anything other than goodness. The moment you understand that, you are already there. All you need to do after becoming aware of it is to practice it.

Once you allow yourself to know in the depths of your being that judgment, punishment, hatred, cruelty, and violence will never lead to anything else, then you can always return to that experience within yourself, which is peace. When other people fail to meet your standards, or you fail to meet your own standards, or life fails to meet your standards, and those strong feelings of judgment, punishment, and so on start to arise, you can go back to that deeper place of peace instead of thrashing around in all this negativity that cannot lead to anything you want.

This is not denying any feelings. It is possible to allow hatred and cruelty to arise, to see them for what they are, and to come back to what you are seeking, which is that deeper place of peace. And you can go so deeply into the feelings that you go right through them to what exists underneath them, to what contains them.

How do you do this? One time you will just be so centered that you go right into whatever is happening and through it to the other side. Another time you will skulk around the edges and sneak in through the back door. It doesn't matter; you need have no pride in this; do whatever will work — just get there. The important thing, no matter what happens, is not to forget who you are — who you *really* are. ◆

Trying To Be Human

This idea says a lot to me: "We are not human beings trying to be spiritual, we are spiritual beings trying to be human." That is one way of describing the illusion we suffer with, the fundamental illusion about who we are.

When we are human beings trying to be spiritual, we are trapped in the illusion; we believe the content of our lives, and our beliefs never make it into conscious awareness so we can examine them and see the illusion for what it is.

But when we realize that we are spiritual beings trying to be human, we are not fooled by the illusion; we have a sense of well-being because we know that life is like a play we are participating in. We know that when we are angry at someone, it does not mean there is something wrong with that person — or something wrong with us for having strong feelings. The anger is simply an opportunity to see how it all works, and to let it be.

When we glimpse this view of life, we may experience a sudden awareness that there is nothing wrong. Everything is fine, and this is home, and I belong here, and nothing is going to hurt me.

Each time we come back to that awareness, it becomes more and more familiar.

And the more we practice, the more that happens. That is the argument for practicing all the time. ◆

Lightening Up

In spiritual practice, your best friend will be your sense of humor. Only egocentricity takes things so seriously. Anytime you can see a little lightness, a little levity, in all this, it can be truly helpful.

So, as you are noodling your way through meditation with your brows knotted, really working at enlightenment, keep in mind the expression "lighten up." It's a big part of enlightenment. ♦

No Hurry

It seems to me that spiritual practice is not something you want to delay. But, once you are on the path, there is no particular rush to get to the finish line.

When someone asked me recently if there is a finite amount of suffering to work our way through, I had to say that I have no evidence that it is finite. And for me, that's wonderful. I love spiritual practice. I love the process. I love wandering away from being centered just so I can come back.

When we can bring some aspect of ourselves that seems unacceptable into acceptance, when we can bring suffering into the joy of the present moment to be healed and released, why would we want to be finished with that? How could we know the bondage of our egocentricity and not want to participate in our own liberation? That's all this practice is: freeing ourselves, again and again and again.

I have a grandson I don't see as often as I would like to — until I see him, and then there are moments, since he's at an age where he's almost as obnoxious as he is adorable, when I feel I may be seeing him more than I want to. Now, I think about egocentricity the way I think about my grandson, in that I can't imagine reaching a point where I would wish that he didn't need anything from me. The idea of finishing with this practice brings to mind an image of being with my grandson as an infant and I would feed him once and that would be it: now that's over! — or hold him once: finished with that! When we know the experience of bringing our suffering into our compassion, we no longer want that suffering to be finished, because that very process of opening our hearts is the experience of love and joy that we long for.

So, I don't ever want to be finished — first, because I love doing this practice, and second, because I strongly suspect that if I were finished, I literally would be finished, and then I would be of no help to anyone.

Since this particular form of Buddhism (Zen) includes the bodhisattva vow, which is not to enter nirvana until all beings have entered nirvana, what's the hurry? You are going to be doing this until all beings enter anyway. (As someone said, we get the image of Buddhists bowing to each other at the door to nirvana: "After you." "No, no — after you.")

It is good to strike a balance, so that you are not dragging your feet and staying where you don't really need to be any longer, but you are also not wanting to get through with things. "I should be finished," we tell ourselves. "What's the matter with me?" The truth is that I am and always have been finished, I just haven't realized it. The point of this practice is realizing that everything is already completed.

Cleaning house is one of my favorite metaphors. Now, it's

foolish to expect to dust my house once and have it stay dusted forever; by the time I have made my way through all the rooms, the dust is already piling up where I began. There is a constant coming back and starting over and going through it again, starting over and going through it again.

And that's how it is with spiritual practice. As soon as we let go of the notion that there is something wrong with that and there is something else we should be doing, then we can just peacefully, joyfully go about our dusting. Or raking leaves, or paying bills, or making a phone call. Or meditating. ◆

Appreciation is expressed to the following
people for their contributions to this book:
Barry Leibman, Mary Sennewald, Jane Shuman,
the Zen monks and teachers who read the manuscript,
and especially Peter Phillips.

This book was designed by Robert Charles Smith
with typographic and production assistance
from Jane van der Kuil.